COMPENDIUM

COMPENDIUM

C.H. WILLIAMS

What you should bring on this journey

through all these words

CAUTION AND CARE

FOR ANYONE WHO ASKED ME
HOW I FELT

ANGER.

I WANT TO UNDERSTAND.
BUT I CAN'T.

NO MATTER HOW HARD I TRY,

I WILL NEVER
UNDERSTAND YOU.

ANGER.

You never understood me.
        You never even tried.

Perhaps worst, you told me
        you never wanted to

                                            Let Down.

WHEN YOU TOOK MY PAIN

AND SET IT ON THE KITCHEN TABLE

ONE MORE THING TO SUSTAIN YOU

HUMILIATED.

IT DIDN'T HAVE TO BE LIKE THAT

UNGODLY WASTE OF TIME

THAT BROKE ME

INTO

PIECES

AND

IT DIDN'T HAVE TO BE LIKE THAT

BITTER.

You,

   THEN ME

A PERFECTLY GOOD CHILD AND YOU GAVE HIM ANXIETY

                                                    MAD.

A TALENT I INHERITED FROM YOU
        IS THE ABILITY
            TO MAKE PROBLEMS FROM
                    NOTHING

I
  CAN
      MAKE
          THE
              WORLD
                  END
                      FOR
                          NOTHING

I CAN TAKE LOVE
AND TURN IT INTO SOMETHING UGLY

GIVE ME KINDNESS
I WILL
LASH OUT

JUST LIKE YOU

AGGRESSIVE.

ALL THIS FEELING

NOWHERE TO GO.

GRIEF MAY BE LOVE WE CAN NEVER GIVE
    BUT FRUSTRATION IS THE LOVE
        WE NEVER WANTED TO DOLE OUT

FRUSTRATED.

"I WILL STOP REACHING OUT TO YOU.

GOOD BYE!"

IT WAS EASIER FOR HIM TO GO
THAN TO TREAT ME WITH RESPECT.

DISTANT.

I NEVER COULD SURPRISE YOU

YOU KNEW I COULD DO BETTER,

BUT THOUGHT YOU NEVER COULD.

CRITICAL.

You CONDEMN ME FOR THE WRONGS I DID
AT YOUR BEHEST

I REMEMBER WHEN YOU SAID

THIS IS LOVE
THIS IS LOVE

AND YOU THREATENED VIOLENCE
IF I DID NOT LOVE YOU BACK

BETRAYED.

THE WORLD WAS AGAINST YOU

AGAINST US,
IF I WAS WILLING TO FIGHT YOUR WARS

YOUR INJUSTICES BECAME MINE

AND THAT BECAME A WAY
TO COMMIT ATROCITIES
IN YOUR OWN HOME

IT WASN'T FAIR.
NOT TO ME, NOR TO YOU,

NOR THE ENEMIES
THAT FELL.

RESENTFUL.

When I gave you everything

And it wasn't enough

Yelling in the kitchen

Breaking another cutting board
                    against the counter

Breaking my heart

Disrespected.

THE CONTEMPT YOU HELD FOR ME

WAS PALPABLE

TANGIBLE

A REAL THING | MEASURED

IN YOUR VITRIOLIC FLOOD

THAT WAS WHEN | KNEW

TO RUN TO YOU

AND GIVE YOU ALL THE LOVE | HAD.

RIDICULED.

I SAID

        I AM TIRED OF PEOPLE LIKE YOU

        STEAMROLLING PEOPLE LIKE ME

YOU LAUGHED AND SAID

        PEOPLE LIKE ME?

AND TOLD ME I WAS JUST LIKE MY FATHER

INDIGNANT.

When you opened my mail

When you stole my passwords,

                deleted my photos

When you hated the words I gave

           and decided to put

                new ones in my mouth

When you picked at my imperfections

                    until I screamed

And when I asked you why

      You told me that the problem was

            You loved me too much

                                    Violated.

I SHOULD HAVE KNOWN BETTER

BUT I WAS YOUNG,

AND I BELIEVED YOU

WHEN YOU SAID

YOU

WERE

THERE

FOR

ME

FURIOUS.

The way you are with your new family

I seethe, watching your love pour over them

Every time you talk about accepting
          your gay stepson

     I wonder

          Why him and not me?

I want so badly to be seen

     the way he is

               the way you see him

It doesn't matter that you're lying
          that you loathe him too
     I want those words more than anything

Tell me you see me

               as the man I am

                    Jealous.

THE TIMES I HAD NOT EATEN

No FOOD, NO LOVE

You WALKED INTO MY ROOM

MESSY YOU WOULD SCREAM

YES, I WAS

HUNGRY AND UNLOVED AND MESSY

I HIT YOU

WITH A STACK OF PAPERS YOU SHOVED AT ME

TO MAKE IT STOP

I WAS RESPONSIBLE FOR MY ACTIONS

BUT YOU WEREN'T RESPONSIBLE FOR YOURS

PROVOKED.

I PUT HIS NAME IN GRATITUDE

AND NOT YOURS.

HOSTILE.

I WAS PUNISHING YOU, YOU SAID

    MYSELF, MY HEART, WHO I AM

        IT HAD ALL BEEN CONCEIVED TO

            PUNISH YOU

MY IDENTITY, A FINELY CRAFTED BLADE

FINE

SO BE IT

AT YOUR INSISTENCE, I PERSIST,

    AND WIELD MYSELF

        TO PERISH AT MY EXISTENCE

    IS AN HONOR YOU COULD ONLY DREAM OF

STAY MAD

            VENGEANCE.

You and me

What we never could be

INFURIATED.

A BEAUTIFUL DRAMA

THE WAY YOU DREW ME NEAR

AND PUSHED ME BACK

MAKING ME THINK YOU NEEDED ME

TELLING ME I WAS JUST A BOTHER

EVER COMPETING AGAINST MYSELF FOR

A PRIZE

ONLY YOU COULD WIN

ANNOYED.

LIKE A HAND

    ONE TOO MANY TIMES TO A HOT STOVE

FOR WHAT ELSE IS ONE TO BE

    AFTER BEING BURNED SO MANY TIMES

WITHDRAWN.

WHAT I WISHED I COULD BE
WHEN SHE TOOK SCISSORS TO MY SIDE
TO CORRECT THE TWIN SCARS ACROSS MY CHEST

SCARS, SHE SAID

SCARS FEEL THINGS DIFFERENT

THEY'VE HEALED THE BEST THEY CAN
BUT NOTHING IS EVER THE SAME

YOU FEEL MORE THAN MORTALS
WERE MEANT TO SHOULDER

NUMB.

I SEE HOW I LOVED YOU

WITHOUT QUESTION

WITHOUT HESITATION

DISGUST.

PASSION, BUT POISONED

BY SINS INNUMERABLE

HATE.

Sadness.

LONGING FOR WHAT COULD NOT BE

COULD NOT BE

COULD NOT BE

WILL NEVER BE

SADNESS.

THE HOPE THAT YOU WILL TREAT ME BETTER

WITH THE UNDERSTANDING THAT YOU WILL NOT

SUFFERING.

When you told me you would be there

and I held that hope

like ribs hold a heart

Disappointment.

Why, why, why am I doing this to myself

YOU DEMANDED

AND FOR A MOMENT, YOU WON

I FELT MUTILATED

YOUR WORDS, THEY DID THAT

MADE ME FEEL LESSER

BROKEN

AND I ASKED MYSELF THE SAME

Why, why, why am I doing this to myself

LOVING YOU STILL

SHAMEFUL.

You told me

    I could only count on myself

I knew it to be true

    when you stood at my bedroom door

    a coward

    too weak to kiss my forehead

I'm sorry, you said, for yelling

    and you chucked a stuffed animal

    at me

    and closed the door as you left

           Neglected.

COUNT ON ME

    LIKE ONE, TWO, THREE

BUT THEN YOU CAPITALIZED THE "F" IN FEMALE
AND TOLD ME I WOULD NEVER BE YOUR SON

DESPAIR.

The moment I realized
I was nothing to you

When I saw
I was not worth
Two words

When saying goodbye to me was easier
than an apology

Agony.

When you said
my anxiety
was manipulative

AND THEN LET ME CRY
ALONE

Hurt.

IT WAS CLOUDY
        AND I ASKED YOU
    IF YOU THOUGHT I HAD A SOUL MATE

YOU PURSED YOUR LIPS AND SAID MAYBE
    LIKE THE WAY SOMEONE SOFTENS BAD NEWS
            A QUIET WAY OF SAYING NO

AND THEN YOU TOLD ME
SOME PEOPLE
    ARE DESTINED
            FOR SUICIDE

                        DEPRESSED.

IN THE COURTYARD
        THAT YOUR YELLING FILLED

YOU SCREAMED

            YOU
                HURT
                    ME

AND I DID NOT KNOW HOW I COULD HAVE
        BUT YOU NEVER LIE
                    NOT TO ME, ANYWAY
        AND I HATED MYSELF FOR WOUNDING YOU

SORROW.

An invitation to witness my joy
is not permission to take credit for it

My happiness is cultivated
well beyond where you live

It is possible to love a garden from afar
without thinking
you've sown the seeds

Dismayed.

WHEN YOU COULD NOT FOLLOW MY FOOTSTEPS
  BECAUSE THESE SHOES,
                THEY FINALLY BELONGED TO ME

                                          DISPLEASED.

I WAS NEVER GOOD AT GAMBLING

BUT I WISH I WOULD'VE TAKEN
YOUR BET

MY HONESTY FOR YOUR DEMISE

YOUR LIFE DEPENDED ON DECEPTION

AND YOU WERE NEVER WORTH THE LIES

REGRETFUL.

EVERYTHING I NEVER WANTED TO DO
AND I DID IT SO BADLY

EVIDENCED BY MY LIST OF
SOULS CRUSHED

ALL OF WHAT'S LEFT
OF GOOD PEOPLE

GUILTY.

WHEN CONSPIRACY CIRCLED YOU

  AND IN YOUR FEAR

    YOU KEPT ME TO YOURSELF

FOR WHERE WOULD YOU BE

IF NOT WITH ME

        ISOLATED.

All the words I spilled to you

Confidences betrayed
Secrets spilled

All the incentives you needed to be with me

A cigarette on the porch
So we could be outside together
A trip to the store
So that we could talk to each other

Lonely.

To me, irreparable loss

    deep sorrow

To you, annoyance

GRIEF.

WHEN YOU SAID GOODBYE
AND I REALIZED

I WAS FREE

AND I REALIZED

I COULD NOT HAVE STOPPED YOU FROM GOING
EVEN IF I WANTED TO

POWERLESS.

FEAR.

WHAT IF

I

WAS WRONG

FEAR.

I STUCK BY OPINIONS

        PEOPLE

          IDEAS

               LONG AFTER I SAW

          THE HARM THEY CAUSED

                           HORROR.

STEPPING ONTO A STAGE

   AND REALIZING

         I WANTED THE APPLAUSE
   WITHOUT THE PERFORMANCE

   BUT KNOWING I MUST GIVE THE LATTER
         ALL THE SAME

                                        NERVOUS.

CONSTANT CRITICISM
OF PEOPLE WHO LOOKED
LIKE ME

THE WAY YOU TOUCH YOUR TUMMY
ROUND
AND SAY

IT IS NOT THAT YOUR BODY
SUSTAINS YOU
NOURISHES YOU

IT IS EVIDENCE
OF WHY IT'S WRONG
TO EAT

INSECURE.

CLUTCHING A PHONE
IN THE MIDDLE OF THE NIGHT
STARING AT SHADOWS

BECAUSE YOUR PANIC
YOUR PARANOIA
IT RAN OUR HOUSE, OUR LIVES

THERE WAS NO VILLAIN AT MY WINDOW

NO
NOT AT ALL

FOR YOU, IN ALL YOUR POWER
CANNOT BE TWO PLACES AT ONCE

TERROR.

THE MOMENT WHEN I ECHOED
    YOUR LIST OF ENDLESS RED FLAGS

AND REALIZED

THEY BELONGED NOT TO YOUR ENEMIES
                    BUT TO YOU

SCARED.

THE QUESTION
     OF WHETHER, AFTER ALL YOU DID,
IF I STILL LOVE YOU

          KNOWING

          IF YOU CALL

          STILL I RUN TO YOU

DREAD.

THE LOOK ON YOUR FACE

WHEN I TOLD YOU

I WAS GOING

TO REMOVE

MY BREASTS

MORTIFIED.

That, after I tried my hardest
still
you will be disappointed

Anxious.

WHAT IF

                              AFTER ALL THESE YEARS

            YOU FIND AGREEMENT
                        WITH THE OTHERS

WHAT IF
        TO YOU
                        I AM REPREHENSIBLE

                              WORRIED.

I GAVE YOU MY TRUTHS

EVERY ONE

EVERY PAINFUL

PERSONAL

LOVELY

TRUTH

AND YOU TOLD ME

I LIED

INADEQUATE.

No matter what I did

                              you made sure I knew
                                    you could
                                       do
                                       it
                                    better

I moved

        mountains

              but not like you could've

                                    Inferior.

You,

    AFTER I SAID

            NO

HYSTERICAL.

I SOBBED
UNABLE TO BREATHE
UNABLE TO THINK
UNABLE TO TAKE IT

YOUR PRESSURE
                              YOUR CRITICISM

          YOUR LACK OF LOVE

                                   YOU
                                   PURSED
                                   YOUR LIPS

                              AND TOLD ME
                              YOU WERE TIRED
                              OF DRAMATICS

WHILE I SAT
      SHAKING ON MY BED
      TERRIFIED OF YOU
                    AND YOUR GHOSTS

                              PANIC.

The one thing you told me never to be

The one thing you needed me to be

Helpless.

IF YOU WERE

TO BE RIGHT

FRIGHTENED.

SURPRISE.

I REALIZED

   I WAS WORTH FIGHTING FOR

SURPRISE.

MARRY ME, HE SAID

STUNNED.

I DROPPED A GLASS
        SHATTERED IT
        IRREPARABLY

AND HE DID NOT YELL
                BUT SAID
                CAN I HELP CLEAN THAT UP?

                                        CONFUSED.

WE WALK
    YOU AND I

    YOU PAUSE BY A GROVE OF TREES
        YOU TELL ME HOW THE WORLD
        IS FULL OF BEAUTIFUL POSSIBILITY

AND FOR THE FIRST TIME
            IN A LONG TIME
            I FIND THAT I AGREE

                                    AMAZED.

I FOUND A PICTURE OF YOU AND I
    AND I WEEP WITH JOY
    FOR WHEN I SEE
        THE TWO OF US, MEN, EMBRACING

    I KNOW THAT MY HEART WAS RIGHT
    TO GUIDE ME THIS WAY

OVERCOME.

THAT YOU COULD BETRAY ME SO EASILY
WHEN I GAVE EVERYTHING FOR YOU

SHOCKED.

Your childish arguments

you yell,
    mistaking feeling for fact
        anger for logic

and me,
    for someone you could treat so poorly

Dismayed.

Such accusations you leveled

I was so sympathetic to you
until I saw the facts
so strategically hidden

Hidden so that truth, and me,

would not betray you

Disillusioned.

WHEN YOU TRIED TO EXPLAIN SCIENCE

AND BIOLOGY

BUT IT TURNS OUT

YOU KNOW SCIENCE

AND BIOLOGY

AS WELL AS YOU KNEW ME

THAT IS TO SAY,

NOT AT ALL

PERPLEXED.

WHEN SHE TOLD ME

    SHE LOVED ME

        SHE, IN ALL HER KINDNESS

        IN ALL HER BEAUTY

        SHE LOVED ME

AND MY HEART LEAPT

            ASTONISHED.

SHOULD BE SOMETHING LIKE

A NICE NIGHT SKY

OR A SUNSET

OR MAYBE THE BAY BRIDGE
EARLY IN THE MORNING

BUT FOR ME

IT IS WHEN MY HUSBAND REALIZED
THERE WAS A FEDERAL TAX CREDIT
FOR THE WATER HEATER

AWESTRUCK.

HE TEXTED ME AND SAID

  IT'S OKAY TO TELL ME
            WHEN I AM WRONG

SPEECHLESS.

AT LAST

you TRAVERSED A BOUNDARY

I TOLD YOU NEVER TO CROSS

AND YOU WALKED ACROSS IT FEARLESSLY

ASTOUNDED.

WITH A SMILE

    YOU BREW A POT OF COFFEE

AND

    POUR

        ME

            CUPS AND CUPS

STIMULATED.

THE WAY YOUR ARMS
        WRAPPED
                AROUND ME
        A HUG

                        AND IT WAS
                THE MOST COMFORTING

NEVER WANTED IT TO END

                AND THERE WAS SADNESS
                        FOR HUGS NEVER GIVEN

BECAUSE I REALIZED THEN
        YOUR ARMS
                WRAPPED
                        AROUND ME
        A HUG

I DESERVED MORE

                        TOUCHED.

LOVE.

THE RESPITE

THE RAWNESS

THE REASSURANCE

THAT TOGETHER, WE CULTIVATE

LOVE.

IN BETWEEN

    WHEN YOUR SINGING STILL ECHOES

WHEN YOUR WORDS STILL RESONATE

    WHEN YOUR FUNNY

        LITTLE

           SOUNDS

             STILL PLAY BACK
                IN MY HEAD

AND YOU SMILE
    EYES BRIGHT

        AND WAIT FOR ME

           PEACEFUL.

How you stop

        And pause

     And slowly touch my cheek

                Right before you say

        Do you want another cup of coffee

                  Tenderness.

WHEN WE ARGUE

    AND YOU YELL

               FUCK YOU

AND INSTEAD OF FIGHTING

        I WISH YOU SIMPLY WOULD DO

        JUST THAT

                                DESIRE.

WHEN WE FALL DOWN
TRIP OVER BARRIERS OF OUR OWN MAKING

AND ALL I WANT BACK
  ARE THE MOMENTS WHEN WE WERE GOOD

    BECAUSE WHEN WE CLICK
    WE COULD SAVE THE WORLD

  BUT WHEN WE DON'T
    WE COULD SET IT ALL AFIRE

        LONGING.

You BOUGHT A SODA

AND OFFERED ME A SIP

I ACCEPTED

AND THEN DRANK MOST OF IT

WHEN YOU FINISHED IT

I ALMOST CRIED

AND BEFORE I'D FINISHED MY SENTENCE

HOW COULD YOU

YOU HAD THE CAR KEYS IN YOUR HAND

AND WERE ALREADY

GOING TO GET ANOTHER

AFFECTIONATE.

SPRAWLED OUT
    BREATHLESS

                WITHOUT A CARE

      AND YOU JUST LOOK AT ME
        SMILING

             AND SAY

YOU'RE BLUSHING

                   SATISFIED.

"I DID DISHES TODAY."

RELIEVED.

AFTER YEARS OF SAYING YOU DIDN'T UNDERSTAND

WHEN I WAS CRYING
YOU TOOK MY HAND AND SAID

I'M SORRY
THAT MUST BE HARD

WHATEVER YOU NEED, I'M HERE

AND I SAW
THERE IS NOTHING YOU CANNOT LEARN

COMPASSIONATE.

ALL THE TIMES
    YOU LET ME RESCHEDULE OUR CALLS
        BECAUSE I'M TIRED

ALL THE WHILE
    KNOWING IT'S NOT BECAUSE I LOVE YOU LESS

CARING.

I OFTEN THINK ABOUT

    THE TIMES

        YOU WOVE THE STORY

        OF MY LUST

EVERY MAN I HAD FONDNESS FOR

    WHICH WAS ADMITTEDLY MANY

YOU TEASED

    PROVOKED

TORMENTED

        PICKED ON ME ENDLESSLY

      KICKED A DEAD HORSE

        SHAMED ME PUBLICLY

AND I THINK IT IS BECAUSE

        THEY WERE TO ME

        WHAT YOU KNEW

        YOU COULDN'T BE

            INFATUATION.

THE UTMOST CERTAINTY
WITH WHICH
I KNEW

I NEVER HAD TO TALK TO YOU

AGAIN

PASSION.

A WORD THAT MAKES ME FEEL WRONG

AM I DRAWN?
THE WAY ONE DOODLES
IN THE MARGINS?

ACCIDENTAL
AND WITHOUT EXPERTISE?

ATTRACTED.

WHAT I THINK I AM

        UNTIL I OPEN UP OLD NOTEBOOKS

        AND UNDERSTAND

DESPITE MY DEEPEST WISHES
REGARDLESS OF THE GOOD MOMENTS

      IT REALLY WAS THAT BAD

        AND NOSTALGIA CAN'T CHANGE THAT

JUST BECAUSE YOU MET ONE NEED
ONCE
DOES NOT MAKE YOU GOOD

                SENTIMENTAL.

MIDDLE GROUND I'VE NEVER KNOWN

FOR WHAT AM I
                IF NOT ALL OR NOTHING

                AND I WILL SEE IT TO THE END

FONDNESS.

Joy.

When you woke me up
      after I had fallen asleep
      on your shoulder
   and asked if you could stay the night

Joy.

In a motel room
       in nowhere, Pennsylvania

     when in the middle of the night
     I set down my computer
       smiling

Because I knew I started something important
                      to me

    and I knew eventually
            eventually

         that my voice would
         carry far beyond
            the rolling hills
    I knew
   I would be heard

                  Pleased.

After years of waiting

Finally, to watch you undo yourself

  and you complain
words get back to me
      through the grapevine

  and I smile to myself and think

I have no sympathy
      for what you suffer

You brought it on yourself

Amused.

You READ MY WORDS

    AND TOLD ME THEY WERE EVERYTHING

    ALL THE RIGHT THINGS

        SAID AT THE RIGHT TIMES

    IT WAS TO MEET A HERO OF OLD

    AND HEAR THAT IT WAS NOT HE WHO SAVED US

        BUT ME

        BUT ME

        DELIGHTED.

SINGING TOGETHER IN THE KITCHEN
                AS WE SHARE
        AN OVERSTEEPED POT OF TEA

                FORGOTTEN BECAUSE
                    I WAS LAUGHING SO HARD
            AT MY OWN JOKE
        THAT I FORGOT TO TAKE THE TEABAG OUT

                                    JOVIAL.

Music loud

YOUR HANDS ON ME

AND I FORGET THE WORLD

IS MADE OF ANYTHING BUT

YOU

BLISSFUL.

THE MOST DANGEROUS WAY TO BE

    FOR WHEN I AM PLEASED WITH HOW I SHINE

    THERE IS THE RISK

        YOU MIGHT EXTINGUISH ME WITH

        BUT A WORD

                                            PROUD.

HOPE THAT ONE DAY
I WILL NOT THINK OF YOU AT ALL

OPTIMISTIC.

I CLICK MY TONGUE

  NOD

    AND SAY

      SO

WHAT ABOUT THAT CUP OF COFFEE

                          EAGER.

WHEN YOU CALLED ME YOUR SON

    FOR THE FIRST TIME

        WITHOUT HESITATION

    AND WITH ALL THE LOVE

        I HAVE EVER WANTED

ELATION.

To you,
    I APPEAR TO BE A MADMAN
IN MY DARK CORNER
TYPING AGGRESSIVELY
AND MAKING FACES

                    BUT I AM WORLDS AWAY
                        WATCHING MAGIC HAPPEN

                                        ZEAL.

I STEPPED INTO A COFFEE SHOP
THE MORNING I GOT THE MOST AWFUL MESSAGE

THE MESSAGE WHERE HE CAPITALIZED

THE "F" IN FEMALE

AND THE BARISTA, WHO WAS HOT AS BREAKFAST
STOPPED WHAT HE WAS DOING
LOOKED AT ME
AND SAID

NO OFFENSE TO ANYONE WHO HAS
COME IN TODAY
BUT SIR
YOU ARE BY FAR
THE MOST DAPPER MAN
I HAVE SEEN ALL DAY

EUPHORIC.

The understanding

that no matter what

REGARDLESS OF

ALL THE FEELINGS

I HAVE FELT

WITH EVERY INCH OF MYSELF

I CARRY ON,

LOUD

AND LOVED

AND SO, SO ALIVE

TRIUMPHANT.

END.